This Book is Presented to:

_____

With Love From:

_____

To Jordan Leigh,
a boy who appreciates a good treasure,
With love, Aunt Melody

To Melinda, Amy, and Peter,
my treasures on earth,
Love, Mom (HLK)

THE SEA HAG'S TREASURE

published by Gold'n'Honey Books
a part of the Questar publishing family

© 1997 by Melody Carlson

Illustrations © 1997 by Helen Kleczynski

International Standard Book Number: 1-57673-055-7

Printed in Hong Kong

For information:
QUESTAR PUBLISHERS, INC.
POST OFFICE BOX 1720
SISTERS, OREGON 97759

Library of Congress Cataloging-in-Publication Data:

xxxx

97 98 99 00 01 02 03 04 — 10 9 8 7 6 5 4 3 2 1

THE Seahag's Treasure

Written by

Melody Carlson

Illustrated by

Helen Kleczynski

GOLD 'N' HONEY BOOKS

"I'm tired of making sand castles!" Amanda tossed her shovel down on the hard-packed sand and looked wistfully at the curling waves. "If the sun would come out, we could play in the ocean."

"Mom says it's too cold to go in today," said her brother without looking up. "Why don't you finish digging this moat for me? Then we can get a bucket of water to fill it."

Amanda picked up the toy sailboat. "I know, Howard! Let's build a boat and sail to Hawaii — they say the ocean's as warm as bath water there!"

"That's ridiculous." Howard was hunched over like a hermit crab. His nose practically touched the sand as he sculpted a neat tower with a point on top. "Hey Amanda, why don't you go find some seashells to decorate our castle?"

Amanda decided to take Howard's suggestion. He usually had the best ideas — although sailing to Hawaii did sound fun. She walked a short ways up the beach, but there wasn't a single shell in sight. She was about to turn back when she noticed an odd figure hobbling slowly toward her. Amanda froze. It must be the Sea Hag! She'd heard stories about this strange old woman — kids made fun of her and some even said she was a witch!

Amanda had never actually seen the Sea Hag before, and part of her was curious, and wanted to stay and watch. But the rest of her said *run for your life!*

Unfortunately Amanda's legs would not move, and her feet remained anchored to the sand. She watched in wide-eyed horror as the Sea Hag paused just a few feet from her. She was so close Amanda could almost reach out and touch her!

The old woman clutched a twisted driftwood stick like a cane in one hand. In the other hand dangled a gunny sack. Her dark-colored cape snapped in the wind as she poked the sand with her stick to unearth a good-sized shell — a shell that Amanda had missed! The Sea Hag slowly stooped to pluck it out, then carefully brushed the sand off with a gnarled finger to expose a perfect shell. She smiled a toothless smile as she examined her find, then plopped the shell into her bag and turned away.

Amanda stood motionless, almost without breathing. Her feet remained rooted to the sand as she watched the Sea Hag continue to move slowly up the beach, mumbling to herself as she went. Finally, the sound of the ocean drowned out the old woman's voice. Amanda raced back to Howard.

howard actually looked up and listened with interest as Amanda poured out her amazing tale about the Sea Hag. Finally she paused to catch her breath.

"Yeah, I saw her up close once," said Howard. "She's pretty scary, all right. I'll bet she's the reason we never find any good shells. Josh Fuller said she takes them all off to her secret cave to mix up magic potions." Amanda shivered with fear and excitement, or

maybe it was because the wind had picked up. Big drops of rain started to splat onto the beach, and the two scooped up their shovels and pails and dashed back to the summer cabin.

"Hey, you're just in time," announced Dad from the porch. "Old Charlie brought a bucket of clams by this morning and Mom's making fritters. But you two sand crabs better go wash up for lunch."

After lunch, the rain poured and poured. Howard and Amanda played a board game that ended with an argument. Then Mom brought out a big tablet and a box of felt pens and they began to draw. Amanda drew a scary picture that looked something like the Sea Hag, while Howard worked on a colorful undersea picture.

"I need some real shells to look at," complained Howard. "I just can't make the bottom of the ocean look right."

"I used to have an old shell collection when I was a boy," suggested Dad as he threw another log on the fire. "I'll see if I can find them." When he returned, he had an old candy box filled with shells.

Amanda and Howard examined the shells, stroking their smooth, sand-polished surfaces. "These are beautiful, Dad," exclaimed Amanda. "How'd you ever find them?"

"When I was a kid we came to the cabin a lot. I'd usually find a good bunch after a big storm."

Amanda looked out the window at the dark, blustery sky. "Hey, there's a big storm today! Maybe we should go shell hunting."

"Yeah, but we better wait until it stops," replied Howard as he drew a fan-shaped shell into his undersea picture.

"You'll have to wait until tomorrow," said Dad. "The tide is just coming in now, but there'll be a low tide in the morning."

"We'll have to start early if we want to beat the old Sea Hag," whispered Amanda into Howard's ear.

That night the storm howled and thrashed and beat against the little wooden cabin. Amanda could hardly go to sleep. She tossed and turned in her bed just like the waves out on the ocean.

But it wasn't just the storm that kept her awake. Her mind was thinking about the Sea Hag. She imagined the old woman puttering around a dark, damp cave that was full of gigantic seashells and bubbling pots and magical potions.

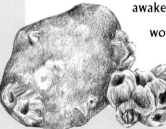

Early the next morning, Amanda and Howard tiptoed outside and fetched their pails. The sun wasn't even up yet, and the sky gave out a strange light, casting weird shadows all about.

Nothing looked the same as in the daytime. Amanda grew uneasy — what if the Sea Hag caught them taking her shells? What might she do to them?

As the sky grew lighter they could see better. And they could see that there were shells! Lots and lots of shells! They had never seen so many sizes and shapes before.

They worked quickly, and soon both pails were heaped. Carefully, they poured the shells out to make a nice little pile.

Up and down the beach they ran, laughing and giggling, and gathering more and more shells.

Their pile grew taller and taller, until finally, they couldn't find another single shell on the whole strip of beach. The morning sun rose and cast its golden beam across the ocean, and the two shell rulers danced around their treasure heap with delight. They whooped and laughed like renegade pirates! They even made up a song.

Shells, shells, glorious shells!
We rule the beach!
Now ring out the bells!

"What'll we do with all our shells?" asked Amanda. It'll take forever to get them up to the cabin, but if we leave them—" Amanda's words stuck in her throat.

Because just then, coming directly their way — was the Sea Hag! And her gunny sack was limp and empty. What would she do to them for taking all the shells? Was she angry? Would she make a bad spell? Howard grabbed Amanda's arm, and together they guarded their shell pile.

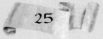

The old woman drew close and peered curiously. She shook her head and held up a crooked finger. But when she opened her mouth, no words came out. Instead she turned and hobbled away.

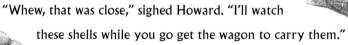

"Whew, that was close," sighed Howard. "I'll watch these shells while you go get the wagon to carry them."

Amanda scrambled up the trail. Her legs felt like two jellyfish. That old Sea Hag had been so frightening! Amanda wondered what the old woman wanted to say when she opened her mouth like that. Was she really a witch?

$\mathcal{T}$ogether, Howard and Amanda struggled to pull the loaded wagon up the rocky path to the cabin. Halfway there, they were met by Old Charlie, the local fisherman who had brought the clams yesterday. As usual, he had a fishing pole over his shoulder.

"Well, what've you kids got there?" Old Charlie peered down at their treasure and scratched his whiskered chin.

"Aren't they beautiful!" exclaimed Amanda.

"Yep," bragged Howard. "We got up real early and beat that old Sea Hag to the beach this morning. And we picked up all these great shells before she even got there."

29

"Hmm, that's a mighty lot of shells. Bet she's feeling purty sad. I know how she always looks forward to the bounty after a good storm."

"You know the Sea Hag?" asked Amanda in surprise.

"Sure, ever'body in these parts knows her. Her name's Mary McDonnel. Her husband was a captain who got lost at sea. Most folks just call her Widow Mary. It's just you summer folks that call her the "Sea Hag", not that she minds none.

Widow Mary collects rocks and shells, then makes souvenirs and doodads to sell to the tourist shops. She lives in that little blue shanty down on the dock road. Selling shells is how she lives." Old Charlie looked at the wagon, then tipped his hat and picked up his bait bucket.

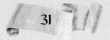

Silently, they pulled their wagon on up to the cabin, then sat down on the porch steps and gazed blankly at their riches.

"I feel kinda sorry for the Sea Hag," began Howard.

"You mean Widow Mary," corrected Amanda. "Me too. I didn't know how important these shells were to her."

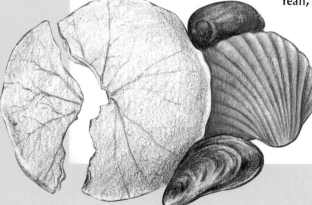

"Yeah, I kinda feel like a thief or something."

Amanda stared down at the huge pile of shells. Suddenly it didn't seem like such a great treasure. She wished the shells would all just disappear. Or better yet...

"**h**ey, Howard, maybe we should take these shells back down to the beach for Widow Mary to find!" said Amanda.

Howard scratched his head. "I suppose.... Or how about if we take them to her. Then she wouldn't have to go to the work of picking them all up again."

Amanda selected a pretty shell. "Do you think it's okay if we keep a few?"

"Sure. It's not like all the shells on the beach belong to Widow Mary."

"I know, but I just want to be fair."

Howard smiled. "Yeah, me too."

They each made a little pile of shells to keep, then went in to eat breakfast. All their early morning work had made them very hungry. They told Mom and Dad about what Old Charlie had said about Widow Mary and their plan to take the shells to her.

"That's a nice idea," said Dad. "I remember Widow Mary from when I was a boy. Even then, some kids thought she was a witch or something. But she's okay. Just a little strange is all."

They both took turns pulling the loaded wagon down the bumpy dock road. Straight ahead stood the little blue shanty.

"I'm kinda scared," confessed Amanda as she stopped to catch her breath. Her hands were hot and sore from pulling the wagon. "I know she's not really a witch. But like Dad said, she's still sort of strange...."
Amanda looked at the house. The roof looked like a patchwork quilt with its different colored shingles. All about the yard lay pieces of driftwood, and parts from boats and ships that had probably washed up to the beach over the years. A strange grumbly growling sound seemed to come from inside. It gave her the creeps!

She looked at Howard and he nodded grimly. She knew he was frightened too. But she also knew he'd never admit it. Instead, he bravely knocked on the rickety old door. A black cat rubbed against Amanda's legs just as the door creaked open.

There in the doorway stood Widow Mary with a puzzled frown. "Hello, children," she said in a crackly voice. Just like a witch might talk, thought Amanda as she nudged Howard. But her brother just stared straight ahead without speaking.

"Hello," began Amanda, her knees trembling. "I—I'm Amanda and this is my—my brother Howard. And we want to give you these." She pointed a shaking finger toward the wagon.

The old woman's eyes opened wide. "Why, thank you, dear. That's very kind." Suddenly, her smile no longer seemed scary. And she really had some teeth after all! The woman stooped over the wagon and picked up a rather plain looking shell. Then she held it up toward the sunlight so Howard and Amanda could see — suddenly it seemed to glow like a precious jewel!

"You're the children I saw on the beach yesterday," said Widow Mary. "Would you like to come inside?"

Amanda looked at Howard. Normally they wouldn't go inside a stranger's home, but Mom and Dad knew they were here. Howard gulped and nodded.

The inside of Widow Mary's little blue shanty was like a treasure trove. Old wooden shelves overflowed with glass floats, huge shells, starfish, colorful rocks, and all sorts of ocean riches. Widow Mary showed them her rock-polishing machine out on the tiny back porch. That was where the strange grumbling noise had come from!

They spent most of the morning visiting with Widow Mary as she told interesting stories about all the different kinds of shells and amazing things from the sea. Finally it was time to go. But first, Widow Mary gave them each a funny little critter created from odd bits of shells and rocks glued together.

"I sell these down at the tourist shop in town," she explained.

"Wow, these are great!" exclaimed Howard. "Thank you!"

"Yeah, thanks, Widow Mary!" said Amanda. "Thanks a lot!"

"Thank you for visiting me," said Widow Mary as they said good-bye at her front door. "And thank you for sharing your treasure with me. And I don't just mean the shells."

"Huh?" asked Amanda and Howard.

Widow Mary smiled. "I mean the treasure of your friendship. That's a very special treasure. And that's worth a whole lot more than the most beautiful shells."

They waved and promised to come back for more visits. Now the empty wagon was easy to pull as they headed back down the dock road.

"I sure like Widow Mary," said Howard.

"Me too," agreed Amanda. "And I like what she said about friends. They're lots better than treasures!"

Don't store treasures for yourselves here on earth
where moths and rust will destroy them
and thieves can break in and steal them.
But store your treasures in heaven
where they cannot be destroyed by moths or rust
and where thieves cannot break in and steal them.
Your heart will be where your treasure is.

Matthew 6:19-21